MW00855960

Prayer

We Speak to God

The Lutheran Spirituality Series

John W. Kleinig

CONCORDIA PUBLISHING HOUSE · SAINT LOUIS

Contents

Hymnal Key

LSB=Lutheran Service Book
ELH=Evangelical Lutheran Hymnary
CW=Christian Worship
LW=Lutheran Worship
LBW=Lutheran Book of Worship
TLH=The Lutheran Hymnal

About This Series

In the West, spirituality is as nebulous as it is popular. Having succumbed to humanism, rationalism, and Darwinism, communities once known for a genuine Christian piety now provide a fertile breeding ground for self-made theologies, Eastern religions, the worship of science and technology, or even a resuscitation of the old pagan gods. In a highly competitive environment, each of these spiritual philosophies seeks to fill the vacuum left by the seemingly departed Christian spirit.

Even among faithful Christians, and at other times and places, spirituality has run the gamut from the mystical to the almost sterile. From the emotional to the pragmatic, the experiential to the cerebral, the all-too-human desire to experience (and control!) the divine has proven to be especially resilient. Influenced by modernism, postmodernism, and whatever comes next, even those who try faithfully to follow Jesus Christ may find defining *spirituality*, or at least what is distinctively Christian about their own beliefs and practices, a significant challenge.

Do Lutheran Christians have a spirituality? Indeed they do! This adult Bible study series explores the rich depths of a distinctively Lutheran spirituality that begins in Baptism and is founded upon God's Word. There, the incarnate, crucified, and resurrected Lord proclaims His victory over sin, death, and the devil, and from there flows the proclamation of His Gospel and the administration of His Sacraments. It is through these means presented within the liturgy of His Church that Christ communicates not merely spiritual energies, an emotional high, a method of reasoning, or a stringent morality, but truly Himself—God in human flesh.

Written by respected Lutheran scholars in the United States and Australia, this adult Bible study series emphasizes the Bible, Luther's catechism, and the Lutheran hymnal as concrete and integral resources for a truly Lutheran spirituality. May God richly bless those who study His Word, and through His Word may they experience the genuinely enlightening and life-giving spirituality found only in the life, death, and resurrection of our Lord and Savior, Jesus Christ.

The Editor

4

Participant Introduction

Since Christian spirituality depends on God's grace, it differs from all pagan forms of spirituality. They all promote spiritual self-development and self-improvement. Christian spirituality is not based on our performance but on our reception from God. We are not producers of spiritual growth but receivers of spiritual life. We have nothing that we have not received from God (1 Corinthians 4:7), who has sent His Son and His Holy Spirit to give of Himself to us. In keeping with this, our praying has to do with our ongoing reception from the God who interacts with us in Word and deed in His means of grace. Our reception has to do with faith, our faith in Jesus and His Spirit-giving Word.

In His three years with them, Jesus taught His disciples, and us, about the close connection between faith in Him and prayer. Before He healed them, He commended the faith of those who asked Him for help. From this they learned that faith was something like the empty hands of a beggar that had nothing to give, but everything to receive from Jesus. Faith in Him, they discovered, led to prayer that received what He promised to give. So when we pray, we live by faith, we act in faith, we exercise our faith in Jesus. We, who are justified by faith in Jesus, have access to the grace of God the Father through Him. We use our faith and our access to God's grace to pray for ourselves and for others.

As disciples of Jesus, we therefore are called to live by faith in a life of prayer. If we stop praying we fall asleep spiritually. We may still be spiritually alive, but we become unaware of God's gracious dealings with us. So He does His best to keep us awake and watchful in prayer. In everything that happens to us God is training us to become people of prayer, wakeful people who take Him at His Word and receive from Him His gifts. God is equipping His people who are sure that He withholds nothing good from us and all His creatures.

To prepare for "Our Secret Vocation," read John 15:9–17.

Cʒ

Our Secret Vocation

Sons are entitled to speak in the family of the Father. Prayer is the permission which God accords His sons to join their voices in the discussion of His affairs.

Peter Brunner, *Worship in the Name of Jesus*, 202

Just imagine that you received a written invitation from the President to join his administration as the secretary of a department in Washington! What's more, if you accepted the offer, you could choose the department that you wished to run. You would be a member of the President's cabinet, having access to the President and all the other people who governed the United States. You would have a say in the administration of this land and would help to decide how its resources were distributed. Think of all the good that you could do!

1. How would you feel about such an invitation? What area would you choose, and why? Under what conditions would you take up the invitation?

Friends of the King

In our contemporary democracies, department secretaries are close to, and assist, the president. In the ancient world, the person who was closest the king, his personal advisor, was called the Friend of the King. He didn't just sit in the royal council; he lived with the king as his secretary, his chief of staff, the man who had his ear.

2. Read Exodus 33:11 and Isaiah 41:8. How were Old Testament leaders and prophets "friends of the King"?

Consider yourself as a member of God's council, his royal cabinet, and picture yourself as an advisor of Jesus. That's what you are. You therefore have His ear. You can introduce others to Him and get help from Him for them.

3. Read Matthew 11:19 and Luke 12:4. Through faith in Christ, how are you "God's friends"?

Grafted In

Jesus develops a picture of Himself as a grapevine and us as His branches that pass on His love just as a branch passes on its sap to produce bunches of grapes. Jesus also envisages His Father as the King of the world and Himself as His royal deputy.

4. Read John 15:1–8. How does this passage describe our relationship to Christ? Discuss Jesus' agricultural metaphor in relationship to our utter dependence upon Him and His willing dependence upon us.

5. Read John 15:9–17. How does the relationship of a friend of a king differ from the relationship of a servant with his royal master? In verses 13–15, how does Jesus distinguish the status of His disciples as His friends from the status of servants? What can they do because they know their "master's business"?

Jesus has taught His disciples what He has learned from His Father. Through His Word He has made His Father's will known to them. They know His business. Work out the connection between bearing fruit and praying to the Father in the name of Jesus.

6. How do we keep the command of Jesus to love each other when we pray for each other?

7. Read Matthew 7:7–12. (Note that verse 12 begins with "so" which is left out in the NIV.) What does Jesus urge us to do, since we are sons of God the Father (vv. 7–11)? In what way does verse 12 conclude verses 7–11? How do we fulfill "the golden rule" of verse 12 by praying for others?

Reigning with Christ

We are united with Jesus Christ our Lord in Baptism, and we now reign with Him here on earth. As priests we have access to God the Father and His grace; as kings we now reign with Him on earth and work with Him in the administration of God's grace. Your area of responsibility as a person of prayer, your department, is defined by your station in life, in your family, your workplace, your circle of friends, and your congregation.

In Revelation, John gives us a picture of our heavenly reign in connection with prayer. The four living creatures are the archangels who represent all the angels. The twenty-four elders represent the whole Church in heaven and earth. As they stand in a circle around Jesus and God the Father, they hold bowls of incense in their hands which symbolize the prayers of all God's people.

8. Read Revelation 5:6–10. For what purpose has Jesus purchased us for God with His blood (vv. 9–10)? How do we reign together with Christ as royal priests where God has placed us here on earth?

The Privilege of Prayer

As members of God's royal priesthood you have access to the presence of God the Father and His grace. Jesus has not just made you a citizen of His Father's heavenly kingdom; He has made you part of His royal family and has appointed you to reign with Him by praying for others.

9. How can you personally use your status as a "friend of Jesus" and your membership in God's royal council for the benefit of those who sin and those who are not yet churchgoers?

Spiritual Exercises

Jesus calls us to live double lives here on earth. We are to live as citizens of this world in our daily work. We are also called to work with God as priests by praying for the people around us. That is our secret heavenly calling, our lifelong vocation (see Hebrews 3:1). Jesus uses everything that happens to us to equip us in this task and to help us become praying people as we grow older and more spiritually mature.

- Make a list of those people whom you are to serve as a priest by praying for them tonight by yourself or with your spouse.
- Begin each day this coming week by praying for the people that you will meet and work with that day.
- End each day this coming week by thanking God for the people that crossed your path and by praying for them according to their needs.

Point to Remember

If you then, who are evil, know how to give good gifts to your children, how much more will your Father who is in heaven give good things to those who ask Him! Matthew 7:11

To prepare for "The Intercession of Jesus," read Hebrews 7:23–25.

℘

The Intercession of Jesus

There is no harder work than prayer . . . But the Christian's prayer is easy, and it does not cause hard work.

Martin Luther, AE 21:142–143

If we wish to be healthy, we need to eat well, exercise often, and adopt a balanced routine of work and leisure. Most of us fail to do just this, so some people who can afford it hire a lifestyle coach to help them to live well.

We Christians know that we are called to pray. Most of us would like to be people of prayer. Yet we fail most dismally in this. No matter how hard we try we don't seem to master the art of prayer.

10. What is your experience of prayer? How do you feel about your successes and failures in this area of your spiritual life?

Problems with prayer aren't new. An early Christian teacher called Agathon said: "I think there is no labor greater than that of prayer to God. For every time a man wants to pray, his enemies, the demons, want to prevent him, for they know that it is only by turning him from prayer that they can hinder his journey. Whatever good work a man undertakes, if he perseveres in it, he will attain rest. But prayer is warfare to the last breath."

11. Why is it that Satan and the demons are determined to turn Christians from prayer?

Jesus the Man of Prayer

Unlike us, Jesus is an expert in prayer. In fact, He is the only expert in prayer—its best practitioner. So He takes over from us and fulfills God's call to us to be praying people. That's part of what He meant when He told John the Baptist at His Baptism, "Let it be so

10

now, for thus it is fitting for us to fulfill all righteousness" (Matthew 3:15). He keeps the second commandment of the Decalogue for us, like the whole of God's Law, by praying for us. Even though each of the Gospels mentions this hidden side to the work of Jesus, St. Luke highlights it.

12. Read Exodus 20:1–3, 7 (see also Deuteronomy 5:6–7, 11). How does God connect His name to prayer?

13. Read Luke 5:12–17. What can we learn from this passage about the practice of prayer by Jesus? If Jesus was the Son of God, why did He still regularly pray to His heavenly Father during His ministry on earth? What does Luke imply about the connection of His power to heal with His regular times of prayer?

Jesus did not just pray occasionally; His whole ministry, from His Baptism to His death on the cross, was an act of intercession for sinners on earth. Luke emphasizes this by telling us that Jesus prayed at all the important points in His earthly ministry.

- Before the opening of heaven, the descent of the Spirit, and His Father's recognition of Him as His Son at His Baptism in 3:21–22
- Before forgiving and healing the paralyzed man in 5:16–26
- Before choosing the twelve apostles in 6:12–16
- Before Peter's confession of Him as Christ in 9:18–27
- Before His transfiguration on the mountain in 9:28–36
- Before the gift of His own prayer to His disciples in 11:1–13
- Before His betrayal, trial, and crucifixion in 22:41–46
- At His crucifixion in 23:34 and as He died in 23:46

14. What can we learn from these examples?

Jesus for Us

God's solution to the problems that we have in prayer is the incarnation of His Son and His life of prayer for us. He did what we could not do for ourselves. Yet His work of prayer for us does not end at His death. Instead, it culminates in His ascension and exaltation as our High Priest in the presence of His heavenly Father. There He continues to pray for all people on earth. He not only prays for our forgiveness, but also for all our needs.

15. What is the truly unique aspect of Christian prayer?

The Book of Hebrews contrasts the ongoing work of Jesus in heaven with the work of the priest at the temple in Jerusalem. The priest interceded for all the Israelites each day as he stood in for them before God in the Holy Place and burnt incense for them, so that they, in turn, could approach God confidently and present their prayers to Him.

16. Read Hebrews 7:23–25. What does Jesus do for us as our High Priest in the presence of the Father? How does He help us by His constant intercession for us?

Carried Along

When my children were young they often asked me to go for a walk with them. When I did, they soon ran out of steam. Then came the part they enjoyed most. I would pick them up and piggyback them. Jesus does something like that by praying for us. In the Divine Service, He comes to us and offers to carry us along in prayer. We, as it were, attach ourselves to Him and are piggybacked by Him into His Father's presence. We join in with Him when and as we are able, but He basically does it for us. He makes it easy for us in our weakness and helplessness.

17. How does the gracious presence of Jesus in the Divine Service and His praying for us make praying easier for us?

Spiritual Exercises

- The common liturgical prayer, "Lord, have mercy," was a beggar's cry for help in the ancient world. Use it as an admission of failure in prayer and as a plea to Jesus to pray for you and to help you in your praying.
- Pray the Lord's Prayer each day as the prayer of Jesus for you and your prayer together with Jesus and the whole communion of saints.
- Use an order of "Responsive Prayer," such as the order found on pages 270–72 of *Lutheran Worship*, as a way of praying with Jesus.

Point to Remember

Therefore, brothers, since we have confidence to enter the holy places by the blood of Jesus, by the new and living way that He opened for us through the curtain, that is, through His flesh, and since we have a great priest over the house of God, let us draw near with a true heart in full assurance of faith, with our hearts sprinkled clean from an evil conscience and our bodies washed with pure water. Hebrews 10:19–22

To prepare for "Gift of Prayer," read Luke 11:1–13.

The Gift of Prayer

The Head of this Body prays together with the Body.

Hermann Sasse, *Ecclesia Orans*

We live in a do-it-yourself society. Authors and speakers make a living selling programs for self-help and self-improvement. These range from methods of losing weight to methods of overcoming cancer. They all assume that if only we adopt the right technique, we will experience success. Even if you go into a Christian bookshop, you will discover pamphlets and books for sale that offer to teach you how to pray successfully and so improve your spiritual life!

18. Why do you think Christian self-help books and pamphlets are so popular? What do Christian materials on prayer assume about the problems we have with prayer?

Lord, Teach Us to Pray

Even though most people pray when they are in trouble, they find it hard to pray regularly even when they wish to do so. That's why religious teachers, including the Jewish rabbis and John the Baptist, have taught their followers how to pray. So it was natural for the disciples of Jesus to ask Him to teach them how to pray.

19. Read Luke 11:1–4. How did Jesus' teaching on prayer differ from other religious leaders in Israel? What was the most important aspect of prayer according to Him?

20. What do you think the disciples expected Jesus to do in answer to their request? What was so unexpected about His response?

14

Jesus gave His own prayer, the Lord's Prayer, to His disciples. This is the prayer that He prays for them and the whole world. By giving them His own prayer, He does three things for them:

- He puts them on the same footing with God the Father as Himself and helps them to impersonate Him.
- In the first two petitions He teaches them to identify themselves with Him as God's only Son and with His mission as the King of Israel.
- In the last three petitions He identifies Himself with them and their needs.

21. What is so odd about Jesus praying for daily bread, the forgiveness of sins, and protection from temptation?

Most of us are too proud to ask people for anything unless they owe us a favor. We would rather do without something than beg for ourselves. Yet we become quite shameless in seeking help for someone close to us, such as a sick child or a needy spouse. God therefore gets us to pray by confronting us with people who make demands on us that we cannot fulfill, people with needs that we cannot meet from our own resources.

22. How do your needs compel you to pray? The needs of others?

In Luke 11, Jesus speaks a parable about two friends, a friend next door and a friend on an unexpected visit. Focus on the dilemma of this person, with an unannounced visitor, and discuss situations where you have felt that you had nothing to set before a friend in need.

23. Read Luke 11:5–8. How is God the Father like the friend next door and prayer like borrowing from Him? How does this parable answer the request in 11:1?

Receiving from God

What's the point of praying? We don't need to inform God about our needs or the needs of others, because He knows them better than we do. We don't need to pester Him, as if He were reluctant to give His gifts to us. We don't need to twist His arm, like a miserly parent, to get a treat from Him. God is, in fact, far more generous than we could ever imagine and far more willing to give us good things than we are ready to receive.

24. Read Luke 11:9–10. What is the point of praying? Why does Jesus give us His own prayer?

In these verses, Jesus uses the passive forms for giving a gift and for having a door opened to indicate what God the Father does for us when we pray. Jesus compares praying to knocking at the door of His Father's house.

25. How do we get more than we ask for when we come to God the Father in prayer?

Best of All

We have, so far, had three surprises in the teaching of Jesus on prayer. Instead of telling us how to pray, Jesus gives us His own prayer, unexpected "visitors" whose needs we cannot meet, and His promise that we receive God and His gifts by approaching Him in prayer. It's all a gift to us. Now comes the last surprise!

26. Read Luke 11:11–13. What is so unexpected about the promise of Jesus in verse 13? How does that promise answer the request of the disciple in 11:1? How does Paul explain the point of this promise in Romans 8:26–27?

Spiritual Exercises

We, naturally enough, regard prayer as something that we do for God by engaging in conversation with Him. Jesus turns that around and tells us that prayer is His gift to us, a gift that involves all three persons of the Holy Trinity. Jesus gives us His own prayer so that we can use it to enter His Father's house and receive Him and His gifts for ourselves and for others. He also gives us His Spirit to help, guide, and prompt us as we pray.

- Pray to God the Father for the gift of the Holy Spirit at the beginning of your devotions and be ready to follow the Holy Spirit in discerning how to pray.
- Make a list of the unexpected "visitors" that God has sent to you and pray for them.
- Follow Paul's advice in Philippians 3:6 and thank God for some gift before you ask for something that you need, so that a sense of gratitude and of confidence in God's goodness displaces your anxiety and diffidence.

Point to Remember

Ask, and it will be given to you; seek, and you will find; knock, and [the door] will be opened to you. Luke 11:9

To prepare for "Praying with Jesus," read John 15:1–8.

Praying with Jesus

One who does not have the Word cannot pray.

Martin Luther, AE 2:19

We learn to do something new by doing it together with a person who knows how to do that task. Boys and girls learn how to cook by helping their mother or father in the kitchen. Teenagers learn how to drive under the watchful eye of a parent or an older sibling. I taught my son how to garden by having him help me out in the garden. I learned to sing by singing together with others.

27. What activities did you learn through the instruction of or participation with others?

That's how we learn to pray. We don't learn it by ourselves but by joining with others when they pray.

28. How did you learn to pray? Who taught you to pray, and how?

In the Shoes of Jesus

The story is told of two British soldiers in the First World War who looked like twins even though they were totally unrelated. They came from the opposite ends of society. The one who came from a good family was married with a young son and had a share in his family's business. The other came from a broken family. The two became the best of friends. The young man with a good family spent much of his time telling his friend about his wife and family. He even told his friend that if he was killed his friend should take on his name and to use it to impersonate him. That's what happened. The man without any family and prospects in life swapped places with his friend who died.

29. How is this something like what Jesus has done for us?

In John 16, Jesus is speaking to His disciples on Maundy Thursday, the night before He died. He explains why He needs to return to His Father through His death, resurrection, and ascension. He speaks about two different ways of praying. There is the old way, in which they ask Him to speak to God the Father for them. It looks like this:

God the Father

▲ asks on behalf of them

Jesus the Son

▲ ask

The disciples of Jesus

But after His death and resurrection they will be able to pray in a new way since they will have direct access to the Father. They will pray in the name of Jesus, in His shoes, as it were, and together with Him like this:

God the Father

▲ ask in the name of Jesus

The disciples

30. Read John 16:23–29. What is so amazing about this new way of praying?

Luther explains what is meant by praying in the name of Jesus:

Christ prayed for me, and for this reason my prayers are acceptable through His. Accordingly, we must weave our praying into His. . . . Through Him we come to God. In Him we must incorporate and envelop all our prayers and all that we do. As St. Paul declares (Romans 13:14), we must put on Christ; and everything must be done in Him (1 Corinthians 10:31) if it is to be pleasing to God. But all this is said to Christians for the purpose of giving them

19

the boldness and the confidence to rely on this Man and to pray with complete assurance; for we hear that in this way He unites us with Himself, really puts us on a par with Him, and merges our praying into His and His into ours. (AE 24:407)

31. Why do we normally end our prayers to God the Father "through Jesus Christ" or "in the name of Jesus"? How does this teaching make us bold and confident in prayer?

Prompting

We do not pray by ourselves, but we pray together with Jesus, who prays for us. Jesus does not just give us His own prayer; He gives us His Spirit-filled Word to prompt, move, and guide us in our praying.

32. Read John 6:63. How are we to use God's Word in prayer? What is the connection between God's Word, prayer, and the Holy Spirit?

In John 15, Jesus compares Himself to the stalk of a vine and us to branches that are attached to Him. He shares His Holy Spirit with us so that we can bear much fruit.

33. Read John 15:1–8. What condition does Jesus put on us in order that we will receive what we pray for from God the Father, and why? How do the words of Jesus help us to pray together with Him? What practical implication does this have from our devotions?

Working with Jesus

By itself prayer is not a means of grace. But when we pray as believers we exercise our faith in God's Word and so use His means of grace. We receive what He offers to us by His Spirit-giving Word and have Him do His work in and through us.

34. Why is this understanding of prayer important? What two pitfalls does it avoid?

In John's Gospel, Jesus performed seven miracles as signs of what He does through the ministry of Word and Sacrament in the Church. These are: (1) the transformation of water into wine (2:1–11); (2) the healing of the official's dying son (4:46–54); (3) the healing of a cripple (5:1–15); (4) the feeding of the five thousand (6:1–15); (5) Jesus walking on the lake at night (6:16–21); (6) the gift of sight to a man born blind (9:1–7); and (7) the resuscitation of Lazarus (11:1–44).

35. Read John 14:12–14. How do we work together with Jesus? What "greater things" are performed in the Divine Service of the Church by faith and in answer to prayer? Why does Jesus emphasize the connection between our faith in Him and answered prayer?

Spiritual Exercises

The praying of a Christian is different from the praying of an unbeliever. We do not make conversation with a god who is silent and remote from us; we join in the conversation of Jesus the Son with God the Father by the power of the Holy Spirit. We pray together with Jesus and follow Him.

- Begin your time of prayer by calling on Jesus and asking Him to teach you to pray.
- Take a promise that Jesus has made, such as Matthew 11:28, and use it to guide you in your praying.
- Begin your time of prayer with a Bible reading and base your prayers on that reading.

Point to Remember

If you abide in me, and my words abide in you, ask whatever you wish, and it will be done for you. John 15:7

To prepare for "Complaining," read Psalm 13.

❧

Complaining

God requires that you weep and ask for such needs and wants, not because He does not know about them (Matthew 6:8), but so that you may kindle your heart to stronger and greater desires and make wide and open your cloak to receive much (Psalm 10:17).

Martin Luther, LC III 27

Most leaders keep themselves aloof from those whom they lead. They don't welcome criticism from them. Imagine a boss who did not just welcome complaints, but actually did his best to discover what had gone wrong, so that he could fix it up. Imagine, too, that he made it easy for his employees to lodge their complaints by appointing one of his senior staff to act as an advocate for them, an ombudsman who spoke up for them in his presence.

36. What would be the advantage of this arrangement?

37. When things go wrong for us and those around us, we get upset and complain about it. Why do we complain? Is it right to be angry with God and complain to Him when we have been hurt?

Daring to Complain

The Bible is full of God's promises to hear the prayers of His people. So, for example, we have this promise in Psalm 34:17, "When the righteous cry for help, the LORD hears and delivers them out of all their troubles." Yet He quite often does not appear to keep His promises. He does not provide for what we need and heal us when we are sick; He does not deliver us from evil and defend us when we experience injustice.

38. How do you feel when it appears that God has not answered your prayers and helped you as He has promised to do? Have you ever felt that He had abandoned you? When, and why?

In Luke 18, Jesus teaches His disciples that they should keep on praying even when God seems silent and unresponsive to them. By urging them to pray *always*, He tells them to pray regularly, *day and night*, as is made clear in verse 7, each morning and evening. In this parable, Jesus contrasts an unsympathetic judge who gives in to a persistent woman with God our heavenly Father who truly cares for us.

39. Read Luke 18:1–8. How can Christians copy this woman? Why are our complaints to God evidence of faith rather than unbelief?

We are reluctant to complain to God because we fear that we will wear out His goodwill and exhaust His compassion. Yet He wants us to dump on Him. That's why He has provided the laments in the Book of Psalms. By giving us these psalms that cover almost every situation, He doesn't just tell us that it is right, and even good, to complain to Him when we are wronged; He actually shows us how to complain in a way that pleases Him. The laments have four main components.

- Complaint to God about what's gone wrong for us, the enemies that have wronged us, and God's failure to provide help.
- Pleas for help from God
- Confession of faith in God's goodness
- Promise of praise for God's help

40. Were you aware that there are more "complaint" psalms than psalms of thanks and praise? How does this affect your thinking about "complaining" to God?

One particular psalm fits almost any kind of trouble and any experience of injustice.

41. Read Psalm 13. How does this speaker feel about God? What does he complain about? What does he ask for from God, and why? Why does he promise to praise God?

Our Ombudsman

In Psalm 22, an afflicted man (David) complains that God has forsaken him so completely that he has been handed over to death and the powers of darkness. Yet Jesus claimed this psalm for Himself as He hung on the cross. He also prayed it for us and all people who have ever felt abandoned by God (Matthew 27:46). He willingly suffered God's wrath for us and descended into hell for us, so that we could pray this lament and all the psalms of lament together with Him.

42. Read Psalm 22:1–18. How does Jesus' appropriation of this lament psalm affect your understanding of how to approach God when you hurt? Besides Psalm 22, what other lament psalm did Jesus speak from the cross?

The risen Lord Jesus is our advocate before the Father, our heavenly ombudsman. He sides with us in our suffering and intercedes with God for us. He does not just pray for our justification; He also pleads with God to "graciously give us all things," those good things that He has promised to provide for us.

43. Read Romans 8:31–34. How does Jesus help us to complain to God the Father? How does He make us daring in voicing our feelings and concerns to God?

Dumping

When things go wrong for us we feel angry; we feel hurt by what has happened and by God's apparent failure to look after us. We either bottle up our anger, which then produces self-pity, bitterness, resentment, and hatred against those who have hurt us, or else we lash out verbally or physically against them. Satan uses our anger negatively to destroy our confidence in God's goodness and to turn us into hard-hearted cynics.

44. How is anger, in a sense, like guilt?

45. Read Ephesians 4:26–27, 31. (Note that the literal translation of 4:31 is, "Let all bitterness . . . be put away from you . . .") We are often told that it is sinful to be angry. How can we be angry without sinning? In verse 31, Paul says that we cannot rid ourselves of anger, but that we need someone to remove it. Who is that person, and how can we get Him to take it away from us?

Spiritual Exercises

- Make a mental list of your "enemies" who have abused you, tell God how you feel about them, and ask Him to undo the damage they have done.
- Use Psalm 13, or any other psalm of lament, to complain to God about your trouble and those who have wronged you.
- Pray "Lord of Our Life" (*LSB* 659; *ELH* 439; *LW* 301; *LBW* 366; *TLH* 258) or Psalm 74 as your lament for the Church under attack by Satan.

Point to Remember

Humble yourselves, therefore, under the mighty hand of God so that at the proper time He may exalt you, casting all your anxieties on Him, because He cares for you. 1 Peter 5:6–7

To prepare for "Praying Together," read 1 Timothy 2:1–6.

CB

Praying Together

Prayer is the greatest prerogative of Christians, which God conferred on them as He placed them, justified by faith, into their filial relationship.

Peter Brunner, *Worship in the Name of Jesus*, 202

Some years ago a minister's conference in the city where I live conducted a survey of the local agencies involved in public life. It set out to discover what they wanted the churches to do in their community. The survey gave a list of suggested possibilities, such as childcare, food aid, shelters for women, housing for the homeless, and so on. When the churches assessed their responses, they found that most respondents had added something that they had not even considered. They asked the churches to pray for them.

46. Why is the Prayer of the Church such an important part of our Divine Service?

47. These public agencies in my city assumed that the Church could make its best contribution to the world by praying for its needs. Were they right? How does the Church serve the world in the Divine Service?

Common Prayer

People in all religions pray to their gods. The normal practice in paganism is individual prayer. Yet we Christians never pray alone even when we pray privately; we pray together with Jesus and the whole Church. Thus Luther says, "never think that you are kneeling or standing alone, rather think that the whole of Christendom, all devout Christians, are standing there beside you and you are standing among them in a common, united petition which God cannot disdain" (AE 43, 198).

48. Read Matthew 5:43–48. How did early Christian worship differ from pagan ritual? What was and is unique about Christian prayer?

After the people who believed were baptized on the day of Pentecost, they devoted themselves to four communal activities in the Divine Service: the teaching of God's Word by the apostles, the presentation of common offerings, the celebration of the Lord's Supper, and the saying of congregational prayers.

49. Read Acts 2:41–43. Why did the prayers of the Church fill everyone with awe?

Paul instructs the young pastor Timothy in how to repair the church in Ephesus. He says that the most important task of the congregation, the thing that it needs to do "first of all," is to engage in communal prayer. This is a "good" thing that "is pleasing . . . God our Savior." Paul gives a simple reason for its importance. God "desires all people to be saved and to come to the knowledge of the truth." So God wants them to pray for "all people." That's how they best serve the world in the Divine Service.

50. Read 1 Timothy 2:1–6. What does this have to say about the connection between evangelism and prayer?

Paul connects the prayers of Timothy's congregation in Ephesus with the work of Jesus among them. The same "man Christ Jesus" who gave His life "as a ransom for all" (v. 6) is at work among them as the "one mediator between God and men" (v. 5).

51. What does the work of Jesus as mediator have to do with the corporate prayer of the congregation? For whom should they pray, and why?

52. Just as Jesus gave Himself "for all," so the Church is called to pray "for all" (2:1). What four kinds of prayers is the Church to offer?

In his first letter to Timothy, Paul tells the Christians at Ephesus to offer prayers in which they would identify themselves with others in four different ways:

- *Supplications* in which they acted as if the needs of others were their needs;
- *Prayers* for the prosperity of others in which they acted as if their access to God the Father and His grace was given to them for the benefit of others;
- *Intercessions* for God to pardon those who had sinned in which they acted as if the sins of others were their sins;
- *Thanksgivings* in which they acted as if the blessings others had received from God had been given to them.

53. Which of these is the most surprising for you? Where, and how, do we do all this in the Divine Service? Which of these prayers do we most often fail to offer?

Agreement with Jesus

Jesus has been teaching His disciples about what a congregation should do if one of its members is lost (Matthew 18:10–14) and how it should deal with one member who sins against another (18:15–18).

54. Read Matthew 18:19–20. Why do they need to "agree" on what they "ask" (v. 19) in this situation? What does agreement in

prayer have to do with the gracious presence of the risen Lord in their midst? How do we commonly voice our agreement with what we pray for in our worship?

Using our Faith for Others

This is a unique story in the Gospels. Usually Jesus healed people who used their faith in Him to pray to Him, to ask Him for something. But this man could not bring himself to Jesus because he was a cripple. So his friends used their legs and *their faith* in Jesus to bring him to Jesus. This is the only case where Jesus healed someone because of the faith of his friends rather than his own faith. They used their faith in Jesus to place their friend before Him.

55. Read Mark 2:1–12. In what ways are unbelievers like this crippled man? How can we use our faith in Jesus for their benefit in the Divine Service?

Spiritual Exercises

When we pray for others, we use our faith in Jesus and our access to God's grace for them. We bring them to Jesus and gain His help for them.

- Remember the people close to you who do not go to church and pray for them this Sunday, either in the Prayer of the Church, at Holy Communion, or in your personal prayers at home.
- Read the words of Jesus in Matthew 5:43–48 and show your love for your enemies by praying for them.
- Recall the people whom you envy and thank God for the blessings they enjoy.

Point to Remember

Again I say to you, if two of you agree on earth about anything they ask, it will done for them by my Father in heaven. Matthew 18:19

Leader Guide

Leaders, please note the different abilities of your Bible study participants. Some will easily find the many passages listed in this study. Others will struggle to find even the "easy" passages. To help everyone participate, team up members of the class. For example, if a question asks you to look up several passages, assign one passage to one group, the second to another, and so on. Divide up the work! Let participants present the different answers they discover.

Each topic is divided into four easy-to-use sections.

Focus introduces participants to key concepts that will be discovered in the session.

Inform guides participants into Scripture to uncover biblical truth.

Connect enables participants to apply that which is learned in Scripture to their lives.

Vision provides participants with practical suggestions for extending the theme of the lesson out of the classroom and into the world.

Our Secret Vocation

Objectives

By the power of the Holy Spirit working through God's Word, participants will (1) rejoice in prayer as a great privilege rather than a burdensome obligation; (2) understand the call to pray as part of their secret priestly vocation to reign with Christ here on earth; and (3) serve as priests together with Christ by praying for the people whom God has placed under their care in their family, social group, and congregation.

Opening Worship

Grant, merciful Lord, to Your faithful people pardon and peace that they may be cleansed from all their sins and serve You with a quiet mind; through Jesus Christ Your Son our Lord. Amen.

Sing "What a Friend We Have in Jesus" (*LSB* 770; *CW* 411; *LW* 516; *LBW* 439; *TLH* 457).

(Focus)

When we Christians think about prayer we normally consider what we do or what we should do. We think about our obligation to pray as Christ has commanded us and our failure to fulfill His command to pray. This topic therefore touches the conscience of every disciple. It can arouse a sense of guilt that disheartens us or the determination for improvement that results in further failure. So a study on prayer can all too easily end up focused on our performance, a self-justification before God and others by measurement of progress in piety.

This study is designed to shift the focus away from ourselves and our efforts at spiritual self-improvement to God's grace and the privilege of involvement in the administration of His grace. The comparison of a Christian to a member of God's royal cabinet is therefore meant to highlight the honor and privilege of prayer.

1. Answers may vary. This initial discussion should lead to consideration of our partnership with Jesus in prayer and His support for us in becoming people of prayer. The answers to this question will

31

vary with the character of the participants. Some people would be honored by such an invitation to govern the United States and be excited by the prospect of improving the way its resources are used. However, most people would feel far too ill-equipped to accept the invitation. They would only agree to take up this task if they could choose a familiar area of responsibility and if they received a high level of support from the president.

Friends of the King (Inform)

2. In the Old Testament, God chose leaders and prophets like Moses and Abraham to be members of His cabinet, His courtiers, His royal servants. As intercessors, they spoke up for God's people and advised God on the decisions that He made for them. They had the privilege of working with God in the administration of His Word in wrath and grace, in judgment and salvation.

3. Through faith in Christ, we are even more privileged than Old Testament leaders and prophets. We are friends of Jesus, the Son of the King, His personal advisors. Yet we have no power by ourselves. We depend on Him for our position and our vocation. He does not just call us to work with Him; He gives us His full backing.

4. By His comparison of us to the branches of a vine in John 15:1–8, Jesus teaches us about our total dependence on Him. We receive everything from Him; we achieve nothing spiritually apart from Him. His description of us as His friends unpacks the practical implications of our total dependence on Him.

5. In a royal bureaucracy with its chain of command, servants did what they were told to do. They carried out the decrees of the king even if they did not make sense to them. The friends of the king, however, differed from them in two ways. They were involved in the discussion that led up to the decision and so had their say in what was decided; therefore, they knew why the decision was made and how it fitted in with the policy of the king. As a result, they could speak for the king and act on his behalf. They did not just work for the king; they worked with him and so shared in his rule.

As disciples of Jesus we are in a similar position. Through His Word, we know what He is doing and why. He has taught us everything that He has learned from His heavenly Father; He has briefed us fully on His Father's policy, His good and gracious will for us and His whole creation. We therefore know our Master's business. We do not merely work for Jesus by carrying out His commands; we work with Him by loving others as He has loved us. He honors us by involving us in His royal work.

6. In John 15:7, 16 Jesus connects spiritual fruitfulness with prayer in His name to God the Father. When we pray we draw on what Jesus brings to us from God the Father, His life and love, like branches that draw their nourishing, life-sustaining sap from the vine. We who receive the love of the Father from Jesus and our attachment to Him are meant to pass on that love to others. We do that best of all by praying for them, for when we pray for them according to God's Word we love them with God's love. Just as Jesus laid down His life for us and put Himself at our disposal by dying for us, we lay down our lives and put ourselves at the disposal of others by asking God the Father to give them what they need.

7. The context of Matthew 7:7–12 is significant for our interpretation of it. In this part of the Sermon on the Mount, Jesus teaches His disciples how they are to deal with sin in God's royal family. They should not use the Law to condemn the sinner (7:1–5), nor should they use the Gospel to excuse sin (7:6). Instead they should use their access to God the Father to pray for the sinner (7:7–12). By the use of "so" in verse 12, Jesus teaches us that we fulfill the Golden Rule by praying for the brother or sister who has sinned. By praying for God's mercy on them we do what we as disciples of Jesus would like them to do for us if we were in their predicament. We therefore can claim God's grace for them and convey His good gifts to them by asking Him to judge and forgive them just as He has judged and forgiven us through Christ.

Reigning with Jesus (Connect)

Each Christian is a member of God's royal priesthood, the priesthood of all God's people. We are all called to serve as priests together with Jesus, our high priest. Our vocation is to reign with Him here on earth as we daily go about our earthly business. We have been chosen to work with Him in administering God's grace by praying for our world. Yet, unlike Jesus, we are responsible for just a small part of God's kingdom here on earth, the area that we know best, our territory, the place where He has put us, our station in life. That's where we exercise our priestly vocation, our area for prayer. We are responsible for the spiritual welfare of the people around us.

8. Jesus has purchased us with His own blood, says John in Revelation 5:9–10, in order to make us royal priests together with

Him. That's our secret vocation, our heavenly calling here on earth (Hebrews 3:1). Since we have access to the presence of God the Father, the heavenly King, we reign with Christ by praying for the world and its citizens. We do so publicly in the Divine Service and privately in our personal prayers. We overcome evil and the powers of darkness in our environment as we use our access to God's grace to claim His help for those who need it and are ready to receive it.

The Privilege of Prayer (Vision)

9. An essential aspect of the Lutheran teaching on vocation is God's call for us to pray for the people in our spiritual care in our family, society, and congregation. Thus Luther concludes the Table of Duties in the Small Catechism with the admonition from 1 Timothy 2:1 to pray for all people. This means that we are not just called to pray generally for everyone, but quite particularly for those that we interact with in our station and daily routine. We should not just pray for their physical needs but also for their spiritual needs. We can use our status as friends of Jesus to intercede for two groups of people. On the one hand, when we discover that someone has sinned, we can ask God to have mercy on them and protect them from the condemnation of Satan. On the other hand, we can note those who are not Christians, or who no longer go to church, and bring them to Christ in prayer for their conversion and salvation.

The Intercession of Jesus

Objectives

By the power of the Holy Spirit working through God's Word, participants will learn (1) to regard their difficulties in prayer positively as an opportunity to learn to pray with Jesus; (2) to give thanks for the ongoing intercession of Jesus for the human family; and (3) to rely on the intercession of Jesus when they go to church.

Opening Worship

O God, the Strength of all who put their trust in You, mercifully accept our prayer and, because through the weakness of our mortal nature we can do no good thing without Your aid, grant us the help of Your grace that, keeping Your commandments, we may please You in both will and deed; through Jesus Christ, Your Son, our Lord. Amen.

Sing "Hail, Thou Once Despised Jesus" (*LSB* 531; *CW* 351; *LW* 284; *TLH* 367).

(Focus)

The devastating effect of original sin is evident in the problem that we have with prayer. Because we are sinners we are "without trust" in God (Augsburg Confession II 1). We therefore find it hard to pray. Prayer seems to go against the grain. We do not like to ask God, or anyone, for help, but prefer to manage by ourselves.

In this session, we consider our difficulty with prayer and our recurring failure to master the art of prayer. We know that we should pray; we would like to pray more regularly, ardently, and spontaneously. Yet the harder we try, the more we seem to fail. And that's how it's meant to be. Christ lets us fail, when we pray by ourselves, so that we will turn to Him and let Him help us out. Oddly, our success in prayer comes from our personal failure and our willingness to let Jesus take over from us.

10. Answers will vary. The first two questions are designed to get participants to consider their own experience of prayer. Encourage people to be honest about their situation. New Christians often

find it much easier to pray regularly and whole-heartedly than old Christians. Mature Christians often go through times of intense prayer followed by arid periods with little prayer. The second question is meant to identify the two main spiritual issues that we face as we reflect on our practice of prayer. First, when we are successful in prayer, we feel good about our spiritual condition and use that as an index of spiritual progress. But that sense of achievement sets us up for eventual spiritual disillusionment when we run out of steam and become slack once again. Second, when we fail in prayer, we feel guilty, and Satan uses our guilt to question our faith or to get us to give up trying to pray.

11. The quotation from Agathon reminds us that in prayer we engage in spiritual warfare. That's why it is so hard to pray! Satan is determined to sabotage our prayers because he knows that when we pray we receive divine help. So his basic strategy is to curtail our prayers and stop us from praying, for whenever we pray, he suffers another defeat and his power is diminished. The more mature we are in the faith, the more we will come under attack because we are more of a threat to his interests. He knows far better than we do that prayer is a spiritual lifeline for us.

Jesus the Man of Prayer (Inform)

12. In the first two commandments of the Decalogue, God gives us His name and tells us to use it in prayer. We, however, fail to keep that commandment, even though we benefit so much from observing it. So God's Son became a man to fulfill that commandment perfectly for us, like all the other commandments, and make up for our failure to be people of prayer. Jesus is our righteousness (1 Corinthians 1:30). The life of prayer that God requires is given to us by our union with Him in Baptism and our faith in Him as our high priest.

13. Luke 5:12–17 gives us a snapshot of the practice of prayer by Jesus. From it we learn that Jesus *often* withdrew to solitary places to spend time by Himself in prayer. Elsewhere, we discover that He prayed in the evening after His work was done (Matthew 14:23), or all night (Luke 6:12), or early in the morning before a busy day (Mark 1:35). Jesus did not pray for Himself, but for the people that came to Him for help. In His ministry, He did not just speak the Father's Word to them; He also brought them and their needs to His heavenly Father. Luke implies in 5:17 that Jesus received the power to heal by staying in touch with His heavenly Father in prayer.

14. The whole ministry of Jesus was an act of intercession for us and all sinners. Jesus did not just speak up for us with God the Father; He stood in for us before Him and represented us in His presence, just as at the temple the high priest bore the names of the twelve tribes of Israel on his breastplate and represented them before God in the daily service (Exodus 28:9–12, 21, 29). Luke's emphasis on the praying of Jesus teaches us three things. First, Jesus prays for us at every stage of our journey with Him from the font to the moment of death. Second, the work of Jesus in word and deed flows out of His ministry of prayer for the people that He serves. Third, our praying depends on His praying for us.

Jesus for Us (Connect)

15. In this section, we come to what is most unique about the Christian teaching and practice of prayer: its dependence on Jesus. The risen Lord Jesus continues His praying that began here on earth. He no longer intercedes for a few people at a time as He once did. As high priest for the whole human family, He intercedes for all sinners in the presence of God the Father in heaven itself. Yet, amazingly, He is also present with us here on earth in the Church. That's where He connects with us and involves us in His intercession.

16. Note that in Hebrews 7:25 the verb for "drawing near" (NIV: "come") is a technical liturgical term for approaching the Father in the Divine Service (see Hebrews 4:16; 10:1, 22; 11:6; 12:22). The Apology of the Augsburg Confession explains this verse in this way:

> [Christ] is our high priest, who intercedes for us. So prayer relies upon God's mercy, when we believe that we are heard for Christ's sake. He is our High Priest, as He Himself says, "Whatever you ask in My name, this I will do, that the Father may be glorified in the Son. If you ask Me anything in My name, I will do it" (John 14:13–14). Without this High Priest we cannot approach the Father. (V 212)

In the Divine Service performed at the temple in Jerusalem, the people of Israel could approach God confidently with their offerings and prayers because the high priest had done two things for them. He had performed the rite of atonement with the blood of the sacrificed lamb to cleanse them from their sins, and he had entered the Holy

Place to intercede for them and to secure His acceptance of them by burning incense before the Lord. Jesus is our great high priest. He does not just cleanse us with His blood so that we now have a good conscience; He now stands in for us before God the Father (Hebrews 9:24) and intercedes for us (Hebrews 7:25). He does not intercede for us in our absence, but ushers us into His Father's presence where He puts in a word for us and presents our needs to Him. Jesus covers us with His righteousness and prays us into the Father's presence. We therefore can approach God the Father boldly and confidently together with Jesus. He helps us in two ways by interceding for us. He leads us into His Father's presence and gives us access to His grace (Hebrews 4:16); He also brings us full salvation from God the Father. We therefore can join with Jesus as He prays for us and our complete salvation.

Carried Along (Vision)

17. We are not left to carry on by ourselves and find our own way in prayer. Jesus helps us out. He does not just pray for us; by His prayers He brings us into His Father's presence and speaks to Him for us. He comes to us most fully in the Divine Service to help us by praying for us. That's why the pastor often introduces a prayer by greeting the congregation with the words, "The Lord be with you." He announces the presence of Jesus as our intercessor, our leader in prayer, and offers His assistance to us. So when we come to church we do not need to worry about how to pray, or what to pray for, because Jesus prays for us. He includes us in His praying and gets us to join with Him as He prays. He therefore makes praying easy by doing it for us and together with us. He offers Himself to us as our intercessor and gives His prayer to us as our prayer.

The Gift of Prayer

Objectives

By the power of the Holy Spirit working through God's Word, participants will learn (1) to pray to God the Father together with Jesus; (2) to respond to the demands of others by praying for them; and (3) to follow the guidance of the Holy Spirit as they pray.

Opening Worship

Lord God, heavenly Father, because You have promised to give what we ask in the name of Your only-begotten Son, teach us rightly to pray and with all Your saints to offer You our adoration and praise; through Jesus Christ, our Lord. Amen.

Sing "Our Father, Who from Heaven Above" (*LSB* 766; *CW* 410; *LW* 431; *TLH* 459).

(Focus)

We believe in justification by grace through faith in Jesus our Lord. Yet all too often we fail to live by faith and grace. In our spirituality and our devotions, we, in practice, all too easily slip back into justification by works.

18. Much of the popular Christian literature and teaching on prayer reinforces the notion that improvement in prayer depends on us, our knowledge, our faith, our discipline, our attitude, and our technique. These works are popular for all sorts of reasons. They are practical and helpful. They feed on our guilt and offer to allay it. They boost our spiritual self-confidence and overlook our spiritual impotence. They promise to empower us and to make us experts in prayer. Their basic assumption is that prayer is something that we do for ourselves and by ourselves. They assume that success in prayer depends on our performance, our willpower, and our capacity for spiritual self-improvement. They disconnect prayer from Jesus and His atonement for us.

Lord, Teach Us to Pray (Inform)

19. Even though Jesus assumed that His disciples would pray, He differed from the religious leaders in Israel by teaching little about the theory and practice of prayer. This was not because prayer was unimportant for Him; He was, after all, a man of prayer and an expert in it. The one thing that He emphasized about prayer, repeatedly and forcefully, was the importance of faith in Him and His Word rather than self-confidence. He taught that God-pleasing prayer depended on Him rather than the person at prayer.

20. The question of the disciple in Luke 11:1 shows that he, like all the other disciples, expected Jesus to teach them how to pray (the right method of prayer) and what to pray for (the content of prayer). Contrary to that expectation, Jesus answered the request by giving them a prayer, His own prayer: the Lord's Prayer. He responds to their "prayer" for teaching on prayer by inviting them to join with Him in His prayer to God the Father. Note that in 11:2 Jesus uses the plural form of "you" and so addresses the disciples corporately.

21. We are so used to praying the Lord's Prayer that we are no longer struck by it and our use of it. It is, first and foremost, the prayer of Jesus the Son to His heavenly Father, as unique to Him as that relationship. As such it is remarkable in three ways. First, since Jesus is the only Son of the Father, He alone may approach and address Him as Father. Yet Jesus shares His sonship with us (Romans 8:14–15; Galatians 4:4–6). By giving us His prayer He includes us in His relationship with the Father and allows us to act as if we were Him, dressed up as Him (Romans 13:14; Galatians 3:26–27). Second, by sharing His own status with us He involves us in His mission, His vocation as the royal Son of God. We may therefore identify ourselves with Him and pray with Him for the coming of His Father's kingdom through Him and with us. Third, in the last three petitions He identifies Himself with us and the whole human family by His use of "us" and "our." This is rather odd, for He does not need daily bread, forgiveness, and protection from temptation. Yet He identifies Himself with us and our necessities, our sins, and our temptation. He sides with us and speaks up for us.

22. Answers may vary. Luther repeatedly taught that our neediness teaches us to pray. He says,

> People must feel their distress, and such distress presses them and compels them to call and cry out. Then prayer

will be made willingly, as it ought to be. People will need no teaching about how to prepare for it and to reach the proper devotion. . . . We all have enough things that we lack. The great problem is that we do not feel or recognize this. (Large Catechism 3:26–27)

23. After giving the disciples His own prayer, Jesus answers their request for teaching on prayer with the parable of an unexpected visitor (Luke 11:5–8). In it He, rather ironically, compares God the Father with a grumpy friend next door. Like the person in that parable we are often confronted by needy friends seeking help from us. Like that person we have nothing to set before them. But we do have access to God the Father, who has what we lack. We can borrow from Him by praying persistently for them. So Jesus teaches us to pray by sending needy people into our lives, people who expose our own poverty, people that God alone can help.

Receiving from God (Connect)

24. In Luke 11:9–10, Jesus teaches us the point of praying. Here, as in 11:1, He uses the plural "you." In Matthew 6:7–8, He tells us that we don't need to use prayer to wear God down by pestering Him or to inform Him about what we need. The point of prayer is to receive from God. Jesus gives us His own prayer so that we can use it and our faith in Him to receive the good things that He has promised to give us. We cash in His promises in prayer. Jesus teaches us how to pray by promising that God will give us what we ask for when we pray His prayer for ourselves and for others.

25. Luther reminds us in the Small Catechism that we pray because God the Father "has commanded us to pray . . . and has promised to hear us" (Small Catechism III 21). His promise teaches us that we pray in order to receive from God the Father. Yet, when we pray together with Jesus we get much more than we ever ask for, "far more abundantly than all that we ask or think" (Ephesians 3:20). Jesus explains this by comparing prayer to knocking at the door of His Father's house. When we knock at the door of our parents' house, they don't ask us what we want; they invite us in. Like our earthly parents, God the Father opens the door for us when we come to ask Him for something and lets us in. We therefore don't just get something from God when we pray; we receive the Father Himself, His company, and life with Him. That is the unexpected bonus of prayer!

Best of All (Vision)

26. The last part of Jesus' teaching on prayer in Luke 11 contains the biggest surprise of all. When He contrasts the willingness of bad parents to give good gifts to their children, we would expect Him to mention God's even greater readiness to give good gifts to us His children, as He does in Matthew 7:9–11. Instead, He speaks about the Father's giving of His Holy Spirit to those who ask for His Spirit. Superficially, this promise of the Spirit seems to have nothing whatsoever to do with the request for teaching on the practice of prayer. Yet at a deeper theological level, it has everything to do with the practice of prayer. Here, Jesus recognizes that the basic problem for us is our human weakness, our spiritual impotence, our inability to pray as we wish and as God requires. His solution to that problem is the provision of the Holy Spirit as our helper, the one who prompts and empowers us to pray.

Paul explains this promise more fully in Romans 8:26–27 by teaching us that even though we do not know how to pray or what to pray for, the Holy Spirit helps us in our weakness and intercedes for us deep inside us in accordance with God's good and gracious will. So when we pray, we can follow His urging, His prompting, even if it is evident only in sighing and groaning and deep distress. The Holy Spirit is the Spirit of prayer. The Holy Spirit is, as Zechariah 12:10 prophecies, "the Spirit of grace and pleas for mercy," the Spirit who gives us faith in the grace of our heavenly Father and who lays claim to that grace for us in prayer. The Holy Spirit assures us that we are sons of God quite practically by getting us to pray to God as our Father together with Jesus (Romans 8:14–17; Galatians 4:4–7). So the best help that Jesus gives to us for our practice of prayer is His Holy Spirit. By prayer we receive the Holy Spirit who, in turn, makes us people of prayer.

Praying with Jesus

Objectives

By the power of the Holy Spirit working through God's Word, participants will (1) approach God the Father in prayer with faith in Jesus as their intercessor; (2) rely on the guidance of God's Word in their prayers; and (3) ask Him to do His work through them.

Opening Worship

Almighty God, since You have granted us the favor to call on You with one accord and have promised that where two or three are gathered together in the name of Jesus He is there in the midst of them, fulfill the prayers of Your servants, granting us in this world knowledge of Your truth and in the world to come life everlasting; through Jesus Christ, our Lord. Amen.

Sing "Jehovah, Let Me Now Adore You" (*CW* 189; *LW* 446; *TLH* 21).

(Focus)

The last session explored the biblical teaching on the gift of prayer. We learned how Jesus invites us to join with Him as He prays for us and the whole human family. This session examines how Jesus gives us His name and His Word to include us in His praying. The first two questions are meant to explore the experience of participants in learning how to pray.

27. We learn most important things in life by copying what others are doing. That is how we learn to cook, to drive, to garden, and to speak and sing. We teach our children to pray by praying for them and with them.

28. Allow participants to discuss their experiences. Most people learn to pray by participating in family prayers, congregational prayer, and bedtime prayer. They learn to pray from their parents and other members of the family as well as from their pastors and teachers. This usually involves joining in set prayers, such as the Lord's Prayer and table grace, and memorizing them by repeated use. We

learn to pray by joining in with others. They hand on the gift of prayer to us by praying with us.

In the Shoes of Jesus (Inform)

29. The soldier who impersonated his friend did not just take on the identity of his friend. With his name he received much more from him—membership in a family with loving parents and siblings, a loving wife and son, part of the family business and the social status that went with it. All this became his at the death of his friend by his word and the gift of his name.

Jesus has done something far greater than that by His incarnation and His sacrificial death. He involves us in a great exchange, His swap with us. In His Baptism, He takes on our sin and guilt, our death and damnation; in our Baptism, He gives us His place with God the Father and His status as the only Son of the Father. He offers all that He is and has to us. From Him we get a new self and a new life.

30. In Christ, we receive a new way of praying that is contained in the Lord's Prayer. Jesus describes this new way of praying as asking the Father in His name (John 14:13; 15:16; 16:23, 24, 26). In John 16:23–29, Jesus speaks about the old way of praying in which His disciples did not have access to God the Father and His grace. They therefore asked Jesus to put their requests to Him. By His death and His return to the Father, Jesus provided a new way of praying that was symbolized at His death by the splitting of the curtain of the temple (Matthew 27:51). After His ascension, Jesus' disciples could use His name to approach the Father directly in prayer together with Jesus. As St. Paul says in Ephesians 2:18, "For through Him [Jesus] we both have access in one Spirit to the Father." The most remarkable thing about this new way of praying is that it overcomes our anxiety about our performance and acceptability. God hears our prayers as if they came from the mouth of Jesus. He is just as pleased with us and our prayers as with Jesus and His prayers. He listens to us as we are in Jesus, dressed up in Him and all His qualities.

Luther's explanation continues:

> What greater honor could be paid us than this, that our faith in Christ entitles us to be called His brethren and coheirs, that our prayer is to be like His, that there is really no difference except that our prayers must originate

in Him and be spoken in His name. . . . Aside from this, He makes us equal to Himself in all things; His and our prayer must be one, just as His body is ours and His members are ours. (AE 24:407)

31. In keeping with this teaching we normally address our prayers to God the Father. We may, of course, also pray to Jesus and to the Holy Spirit. But that's not the normal way. We conclude our prayers to God the Father by saying that we pray "through Jesus Christ" or "in the name of Jesus." We thereby acknowledge that we pray together with Jesus who intercedes for us and leads us in our prayers. We use the name of Jesus and our faith in Him to approach the Father with a good conscience, without fear of condemnation and rejection by Him. This teaching makes us bold in prayer for two reasons. We need not be anxious about whether God is pleased with us and whether He will give us a favorable hearing (see 1 John 3:21–22; 4:13–15). We need not worry about what to pray for, and how, because Jesus covers us with His righteousness and perfects our prayers. Our performance does not matter; everything depends on Jesus and our faith in Him.

Prompting (Connect)

32. Jesus did not just give us God's Word to be preached and taught; He gave it to be used in prayer and praise. His Word differs from human speech because it is "spirit and life" (John 6:63). Since His words are inspired by the Holy Spirit, they bring the Holy Spirit to us and fill us with the Holy Spirit. In the Smalcald Articles, Luther therefore asserts, "God grants His Spirit or grace to no one except through or with the preceding outward Word" (III VIII 3). Jesus helps us to pray together with Him by giving us His Word and His Holy Spirit with His Word. So when we use His Word to pray, we pray by the Spirit.

33. In John 15:1–8, Jesus teaches us that prayer is the key to spiritual fruitfulness. He does not refer to just any kind of prayer, but only to prayer that comes from union with Jesus. There is one important condition for fruitful prayer. Our praying must echo the words of Jesus that remain in us. His words teach us to pray and prompt us as we pray. We therefore pray, as Luther so often tells us, in obedience to God's Word, His commands and promises, because through His Word we remain in Jesus and He remains in us. When His words

remain in us, they move and empower us with His Holy Spirit. The more the words of Jesus dwell in us, the more they transform our wishes and desires so that they are in tune with the will of God and with the intercession of Jesus (1 John 5:14). The Father will give us whatever we wish because we will desire what He wants to give us. This has far-reaching implications for the practice of prayer. In our Lutheran tradition, we usually begin our devotions with the reading of God's Word and meditation on it so that His Word can prompt us as we pray. We pray in accordance with His commands and promises, because they harmonize with the intercession of Jesus and synchronize us with the intercession of the Holy Spirit in us.

Working with Jesus (Vision)

34. Even though God commands us to pray and promises to hear us when we pray to Him in the name of Jesus, prayer is not a means of grace. When we pray in the name of Jesus, we exercise our faith in God's Word and rely on it as our means of grace. In prayer we, by faith, receive what God gives us through His Word. In prayer, God does His work in and through us who trust in His Word.

35. The understanding of prayer is important because it avoids two pitfalls in our thinking about prayer: prayer is our act that we do apart from God's Word, or genuine prayer can be made apart from faith in God's Word. In John 14:12–14, Jesus says that we work together with Him by praying to the Father in His name. The *greater things* performed by the disciples are the "miracles" that are worked by baptizing, preaching, and celebrating the Lord's Supper. Jesus emphasizes the importance of faith in doing His work because by ourselves we have no power to do God's work; we are totally dependent on Christ and His Word. He does His work in and through us as we use our faith in Him to ask the Father for everything.

Complaining

Objectives

By the power of the Holy Spirit working through God's Word, participants will (1) acknowledge their anger at what has gone wrong for them; (2) complain to God about His treatment of them; and (3) appeal to His grace in the face of His apparent wrath.

Opening Worship

Almighty and everlasting God, the consolation of the sorrowful and the strength of the weak, may the prayers of those who in any tribulation or distress cry out to You graciously come before You, so that in all their necessities they may mark and receive Your manifold help and comfort; through Jesus Christ our Lord. Amen.

Sing "With the Lord Begin Your Task" (*LSB* 869; *ELH* 82; *CW* 478; *LW* 483; *LBW* 444; *TLH* 540).

(Focus)

36. We do not need to be taught how to complain. It comes naturally to us. When something goes wrong for us, or when we feel that we have been wronged, we complain. And that's good. By complaining we let off steam; we don't cover up the hurt and bottle up our anger, but rather deal with what has happened to us. Yet we seldom complain directly to anyone who could fix it up for us. Instead, we sound off to those around us and take it out on them. The advantage of an ombudsman in a workplace is that employees actually have someone to fix up what has gone wrong, discreetly, without resorting to the law and causing further alienation.

37. There are many reasons why we complain when things go wrong, so answers will vary. We complain because we need to let off steam, because we feel that we have been treated unjustly, and because we want someone to vindicate us. The last of these is most significant. We want someone to affirm that we are in the right and that our "enemy," the person who has injured us, is in the wrong. Their affirmation helps us to ignore our own complicity in the matter. It proves our innocence and allows us to occupy the moral high ground

47

against our enemies. We may, of course, complain to God because He is our Judge. Yet the answer to the second question is not as important as the consideration of the issue. It is worth noting that many Christians feel that it is wrong to be angry and even worse to be angry with God. They therefore believe that they should not complain to God, but must always put on a happy face with Him.

Daring to Complain (Inform)

38. Popular piety holds that if you are a good Christian you will prosper. Yet our own experience contradicts that expectation. Things go wrong for us. Then when we ask God for help, nothing much seems to happen. Things may even get worse. When God fails to answer our prayers, we feel that He is either not what He claims to be, just and gracious, compassionate and generous, or that He is so angry with us that He has abandoned us. The last two questions are open-ended and are meant to get people to reflect on their actual experience.

39. The widow in this parable has experienced injustice in a court of law. Her "adversary" has been backed by the court, even though she was in the right. But she does not give up. She goes beyond the law and appeals directly to the judge outside the court, because she knows that he is not a stickler for legality and conventional morality. She keeps on demanding justice from him against her "adversary" because he is a vain man who cares for his reputation. This comes out more clearly in the Greek than in our English translation, for the judge does not just fear that she "will wear him down" but that she "will give him a black eye" if he does not consider her complaint. Unlike that judge, God is truly just; like him, God exercises grace and vindicates us apart from the Law. Christians therefore copy this widow by trusting that God will deliver them from their adversary, the devil, and vindicate them. Jesus, in fact, commands them to bring their complaints to God daily. These complaints are evidence of their faith because they assume that, even though God may appear to be indifferent, unresponsive, and unhelpful, actually He is just, gracious, and merciful. They appeal to His grace in the face of His apparent wrath.

40. Answers may vary. There are far more laments in the Psalter than psalms of thanksgiving and praise. The most surprising part in many of these laments is the complaint. The complaint usually goes in three directions. First, the psalmist describes his trouble in vivid

imagery, which is general enough to suit any circumstance from sickness to social disgrace. This focus on trouble shifts to a description of the injuries sustained from his enemies, and from there to a graphic description of the enemies themselves in all their demonic malevolence. Lastly, the complaint is also often directed against God Himself for His dereliction of duty. It is not as if God has caused the evil that has come upon the psalmist. Rather, the psalmist complains that, despite all His promises, God has either abandoned him or else decided to do nothing to help him in his dire need. God has failed to keep His promises. These complaints use anger as a stimulus for prayer. In them God's people pour out the bitterness of their hearts to God and argue angrily with Him. They refuse to accept disaster as the proper condition for God's people and protest vehemently against it. By their vivid portrayal of trouble, they appeal to God's reputed compassion. They appeal to God's justice in the face of injustice, to God's grace in the face of His wrath. Despite their troubles, they assume that God is still involved with them and committed to them. They take God at His word and refuse to shut up until He intervenes and deals with their troubles.

41. The speaker in Psalm 13 feels angry with God for rejecting him by turning His face from him and ignoring his distress. He is upset because God seems inattentive and indifferent to him. Yet he does not blame God for causing his trouble. He complains that God has done nothing to fix it; He has let it drag on far too long. Hence the repeated cry "How long?" The speaker asks for three things—God's attention, an answer to his prayer, and deliverance from the threat of death. He gives three reasons for making these requests—God's commitment to him, the prospect of death apart from God's deliverance, and the triumph of his enemies over him if he dies. By his promise of praise he does not attempt to manipulate God but rather expresses his confidence in God's grace.

Our Ombudsman (Connect)

42. Answers may vary. By praying these laments, Jesus joins with David as he prays to God on behalf of all Israel and all the human family in their suffering. He identifies Himself with our human lot and suffers for us. Thus, as He hangs on the cross, He prays two laments, Psalm 22 in which He complains about His abandonment by God (Matthew 27:46), and Psalm 31 in which He commits himself to God the Father for His vindication (Luke 23:46).

43. These verses need to be considered in the light of Paul's instruction on the intercession of the Spirit in Romans 8:26–27 and his claim in 8:28 that in all things God works for good to those who love Him. Thus, by His intercession, Jesus does not just plead for our justification before God, but also for our reception of all good gifts from Him. Because Jesus acts as our ombudsman and intercedes for us, we can be sure that He backs us when we bring our troubles to God. We can be sure that no matter how much our experience seems to contradict God's promises of blessing, He will bring good out of all the bad things that happen to us. Since Jesus intercedes for us, we can be bold in lamenting and complaining to God because we know that He would have to spurn His own Son if He rejected us and our complaints.

Dumping (Vision)

44. Anger by itself is not sinful, because God Himself is angry at sin, abuse, and injustice. Like guilt anger is a gift of God, the proper healthy reaction to evil. But guilt can lead to sin if it is abused and not used as a stimulus for prayer.

45. These words of St. Paul show us how God wants us to use our anger productively. We can be angry without sinning if we use it in two ways. First, we must deal with it day by day without letting it get out of hand and take over. Second, we may hand over our anger, with its fruits—bitterness, rage, quarrelling, slander, and malice—to Jesus in prayer and unload it on Him. He alone can take it away from us and heal the hurt that has produced it. But He can't remove it unless we acknowledge, release, and hand it over to Him. So then, God uses our anger to teach us to complain to Him and to pray for help from Him.

Praying Together

Objectives

By the power of the Holy Spirit working through God's Word, participants will (1) understand their involvement in the Prayer of the Church; (2) join with the congregation in praying for the world; and (3) intercede each Sunday for their unchurched acquaintances.

Opening Worship

We thank You, Holy Father, that You have promised to hear us when we pray to You in the name of Jesus. Teach us how to pray, tell us what to say, and give us Your Holy Spirit to pray for others; through Your Son, Jesus Christ our Lord. Amen.

Sing "O Christ, Our True and Only Light" (*LSB* 839; *ELH* 198; *CW* 569; *LW* 314; *LBW* 380; *TLH* 512).

(Focus)

46. The Prayer of the Church is a vital part of our worship. In it the congregation does not just pray for itself, but for the world and all people in need, no matter who they are. Luther says this about congregational prayer,

> Such prayer is a precious thing and a powerful defense against the devil and his assaults. For in it, all Christendom combines its forces with one accord; and the harder it prays, the more effective it is and the sooner it is heard. . . . Thus it is certain that whatever still stands and endures, whether it is in the spiritual or in the secular realm, is being preserved through prayer. (AE 21:140)

47. There is no single right answer to the first question. It aims to get participants to reflect on their status as justified saints with access to God's grace through faith in Jesus Christ (Romans 5:1–2). Luther agrees with the people in the survey. He maintains that "the true office and function" of Christians is their work of praying for others who have not yet come to faith (AE 24:87). Only believers can do this, for they alone have access to the grace of God the Father. The

Church serves the world best by praying for it and its rulers in the Prayer of the Church.

Common Prayer (Inform)

48. In Matthew 5:43–48, Jesus commands that we pray for our enemies. The worship of early Christians differed from the rituals performed by their neighbors in their practice of common prayer. The critics of the Church were astonished that Christians prayed for people who were unrelated to them, foreigners, and even their enemies, rather than just for their families and their community. This was, and still is, a counter-cultural feature of Christian piety. In the Divine Service, all Christians pray together with Jesus and the whole Church for the world.

49. This practice of common prayer, which had its origins in Jewish worship at the temple and in the synagogue, began with the mother church in Jerusalem. Acts 2:41–43 shows that, from the beginning, all baptized believers were involved in the offering of common prayers in the Divine Service. The people of Jerusalem were filled with awe at their solidarity in prayer. They were amazed that by joining in common prayer Christians put aside their own concerns and focused on the needs of others.

50. In 1 Timothy 2:1–6, Paul instructs Timothy on the nature and function of congregational prayer. The first thing that the church in Ephesus is required to do, in response to hearing the Gospel, is to engage in communal prayer. This does not just please God the Father; it is an essential part of their involvement in His mission to all people on earth. It is the basis for the work of evangelism in their community, for then, as now, evangelism flows from intercessory prayer for those who have not yet "come to the knowledge of the truth."

51. Jesus did not just sacrifice His life as a ransom for all people. He is now at work in the Church as the one and only mediator between God the Father and all men. Since God wants all people to be saved, Jesus intercedes for all people and prays for their salvation. So the congregation, too, joins with Jesus in His ministry of intercession for the world. Paul says that it should pray for two main groups of people. First, it should pray generally for "all people" without exception, because God "desires all people to be saved." Second, it should pray specifically for "kings and all who are in high positions." Whether they are good or bad rulers, they need our prayers because

they are meant to front for God and work for Him in ruling His world. They can't do that without God's help and the prayers of the Church. Paul's reference to kings needs to be translated into modern terms that fit our democratic system of government with its dispersal of powers rather than the Roman system with its concentration of power in a single person. We need to pray for those who work in all levels of government, from the local to the international sphere, because they can either use their authority to advance the spread of the Gospel by promoting justice, peace, and good order, or abuse their power to hinder the work of the Church by unleashing the powers of darkness.

52. Paul tells Timothy's congregation in Ephesus to offer four different kinds of prayer for the human family: *supplications* or *petitions* for them in their need, *prayers* for their prosperity, *intercessions* for those who have done wrong, and *thanksgivings* for those who have prospered.

53. Answers may vary. By praying for others we, like Jesus, identify ourselves with them. First, we stand in for them by our *supplications* to God for them in their need. If they are in trouble, we don't distance ourselves from them, but we act as if their needs were ours. We plead with God to help them in their need, whether they are sick, depressed, unemployed, divorced, or whatever. Second, even if they aren't in trouble we still stand in for them by our *prayers* to God for their prosperity. We act as if their lives were ours. We ask God to give them His good gifts, such as health, success at work and at home, and any other gift available to them in the order of creation. Third, we stand in for them by our *intercessions* on their behalf before God when they have sinned. If they have done something evil, we don't damn them, but we act as if their sins were ours. We ask God to have mercy on them and give them the opportunity to repent. Fourth, we stand in for them by our thanksgivings for the blessings that they have received from God. If they prosper and things go well for them, we don't envy them and begrudge them their happiness, but we act as if their blessings were ours. We use our access to God to thank Him on their behalf for His generosity to them, because they are not yet in the position to do so for themselves.

Answers to the first question will vary with the varied experience of worship. I am astonished by Paul's instruction to thank God for the blessings that others have received. We are meant to pray in these four ways in the Prayer of the Church which is based on this instruction. In it we pray for the world, its rulers, and all people according to their needs. People will vary in their response to the last question, but will, most likely, mention intercessory prayer for evildoers and criminals as the most neglected aspect of prayer in the Church today.

Agreement with Jesus (Connect)

54. The Greek word for "agree" in Matthew 18:19 means that we are to speak with one voice, a common voice. Here, Jesus does not just stress the importance of common congregational prayer; He maintains that it depends on our agreement in a common confession of faith, and our verbal assent to the content of our liturgical prayers. If we disagree with what is prayed for, we don't just dissociate ourselves from the congregation but also disagree with Christ who leads us in prayer. Through our agreement with each other and Jesus in our common prayers, the Father does His work among us and through us. We most commonly voice our agreement and assent with the use of the Hebrew acclamation "Amen." By its use we pray together with one voice, the voice of Jesus.

Using our Faith for Others (Vision)

55. This story in Mark 2:1–12 illustrates what we do when we pray for unbelievers. We use our faith in Jesus to bring them to Him. Unbelievers are like this crippled man because they cannot approach God with a good conscience, since they do not yet have faith and have not yet received forgiveness. They may wish to get help from Him, but they lack the ability to come to Him. Faith gives us legs to walk in the way of the Lord. As believers we use our faith in Jesus and our access to the Father's grace for the benefit of others by praying for them. We do this corporately in the Prayer of the Church. We bring them with us to church and place them before Jesus by interceding for them.

Appendix of Lutheran Teaching

Below you will find examples of how the first Lutherans addressed the issues of prayer. They will help you understand this important aspect of Lutheran spirituality.

Putting His Words in Our Mouths

The first Lutherans took great pains to distinguish prayer as a God-pleasing good work of a justified person from prayer as a good work that earned God's approval. They emphasized three things. First, Christian prayer depends on God's commands and promises rather than the performance of the person, for by His Word God gives access to His grace. The power of prayer therefore comes from God's Spirit-filled Word. Second, prayer is an act of faith by which a believer receives a good conscience before God and all His promised gifts. Third, Christ encourages and helps His disciples to pray by giving them the Lord's Prayer. God therefore "expects us and He Himself arranges the words and form of prayer for us. He places them on our lips for how and what we should pray" (Large Catechism III 22).

Small Catechism III

Our Father who art in heaven.

What does this mean?

Answer: By these words God would tenderly encourage us to believe that He is our true Father and that we are His true children, so that we may ask Him confidently with all assurance, as dear children ask their dear father. (1–2)

Amen.

What does this mean?

Answer: I should be certain that these petitions are acceptable to our Father in heaven and are heard by Him. For He Himself has commanded us to pray this way and has promised that He will hear us. Amen, Amen; that is, "Yes, yes, it shall be so." (21)

Large Catechism III

We have now heard what we must do and believe, in what things the best and happiest life consists. Now follows the third part, how we ought to pray. For we are in a situation where no person can perfectly keep the Ten Commandments, even though he has begun to believe. The devil with all his power, together with the world and our own flesh, resists our efforts. Therefore, nothing is more necessary than that we should continually turn towards God's ear, call upon Him, and pray to Him. We must pray that He would give, preserve, and increase faith in us and the fulfillment of the Ten Commandments (2 Thessalonians 1:3). We pray that He would remove everything that is in our way and that opposes us in these matters. So that we might know what and how to pray, our Lord Christ has Himself taught us both the way and the words (Luke 11:1–4), as we shall see.

But before we explain the Lord's Prayer part by part, it is most necessary first to encourage and stir people to prayer, as Christ and the apostles also have done (Matthew 6:5–15). And the first thing to know is that it is our duty to pray because of God's commandment. For that's what we heard in the Second Commandment, "You shall not take the name of the LORD your God in vain" (Exodus 20:7). We are required to praise that holy name and call upon it in every need, or to pray. To call upon God's name is nothing other than to pray (e.g., 1 Kings 18:24). Prayer is just as strictly and seriously commanded as all other commandments: to have no other God, not to kill, not to steal, and so on. Let no one think that it makes no difference whether he prays or not. Common people think this, who grope in such delusion and ask, "Why should I pray? Who knows whether God heeds or will hear my prayer? If I do not pray, someone else will." And so they fall into the habit of never praying. They build a false argument, as though we taught that there is no duty or need for prayer, because we reject false and hypocritical prayers (Matthew 6:5). (1–6)

But praying, as the Second Commandment teaches, is to call upon God in every need. He requires this of us and has not left it to our choice. But it is our duty and obligation to pray, if we would be Christians, just as it is our duty and obligation to obey our parents and the government. For by calling upon God's name and praying, His name is honored and used well. This you must note above all things, so that you may silence and reject thoughts that would keep and deter us from prayer. It would be useless for a son to say to his father, "What good does my obedience do me? I will go and do what I can. It makes no difference." But there stands the commandment, "You shall and must obey." So here prayer is not left to my will to do it or leave it undone, but it shall and must be offered at the risk of God's wrath and displeasure.

This point is to be understood and noted before everything else. Then by this point we may silence and cast away the thoughts that would keep and deter us from praying, as though it does not matter if we do not pray, or as though prayer was commanded for those who are holier and in better favor with God than we are. Indeed, the human heart is by nature so hopeless that it always flees from God and imagines that He does not wish or desire our prayer, because we are sinners and have earned nothing but wrath (Romans 4:15). Against such thoughts (I say), we should remember this commandment and turn to God, so that we may not stir up His anger more by such disobedience. For by this commandment God lets us plainly understand that He will not cast us away from Him or chase us away (Romans 11:1). This is true even though we are sinners. But instead He draws us to Himself (John 6:44), so that we might humble ourselves before Him (1 Peter 5:6), bewail this misery and plight of ours, and pray for grace and help (Psalm 69:13). Therefore, we read in the Scriptures that He is also angry with those who were punished for their sin, because they did not return to Him and by their prayers turn away His wrath and seek His grace (Isaiah 55:7).

Now, from the fact that prayer is so solemnly commanded, you are to conclude and think that no one should in any way despise his prayer. Instead, he should count on prayer.

He should always turn to an illustration from the other commandments. A child should in no way despise his obedience to father and mother, but should always think, "This work is a work of obedience. What I do I do for no other reason than that I may walk in the obedience and commandment of God. On this obedience I can settle and stand firm, and I can value it as a great thing, not because of my worthiness, but because of the commandment." So here also, we should think about the words we pray and the things we pray for as things demanded by God and done in obedience to Him. We should think, "On my account this prayer would amount to nothing. But it shall succeed, because God has commanded it." Therefore, everybody—no matter what he has to say in prayer—should always come before God in obedience to this commandment. (8–13)

For we let thoughts like these lead us astray and stop us: "I am not holy or worthy enough. If I were as godly and holy as St. Peter or St. Paul, then I would pray." But put such thoughts far away. For the same commandment that applied to St. Paul applies also to me. The Second Commandment is given as much on my account as on his account, so that Paul can boast about no better or holier commandment.

You should say, "My prayer is as precious, holy, and pleasing to God as that of St. Paul or of the most holy saints. This is the reason: I will gladly grant that Paul is personally more holy, but that's not because of the commandment. God does not consider prayer because of the person, but because of His Word and obedience to it. For I rest my prayer on the same commandment on which all the saints rest their prayer. Furthermore, I pray for the same thing that they all pray for and always have prayed. Besides, I have just as great a need of what I pray for as those great saints; no, even a greater one than they."

Let this be the first and most important point, that all our prayers must be based and rest upon obedience to God, regardless of who we are, whether we are sinners or saints, worthy or unworthy. We must know that God will not have our prayer treated as a joke. But He will be angry and punish all who do not pray, just as surely as He punishes all other disobedience. Furthermore, He will not allow our prayers to be in vain or lost. For if He did not intend to answer your prayer, He would not ask you to pray and add such a severe commandment to it.

In the second place, we should be more encouraged and moved to pray because God has also added a promise and declared that it shall surely be done for us as we pray. He says in Psalm 50:15, "Call upon Me in the day of trouble; I will deliver you." And Christ says in the Gospel of St. Matthew, "Ask, and it will be given to you; . . . for everyone who asks receives" (7:7–8). Such promises certainly ought to encourage and kindle our hearts to pray with pleasure and delight. For He testifies with His own Word that our prayer is heartily pleasing to Him. Furthermore, it shall certainly be heard and granted, in order that we may not despise it or think lightly of it and pray based on chance.

You can raise this point with Him and say, "Here I come, dear Father, and pray, not because of my own purpose or because of my own worthiness. But I pray because of Your commandment and promise, which cannot fail or deceive me." Whoever, therefore, does not believe this promise must note again that he outrages God like a person who thoroughly dishonors Him and accuses Him of falsehood.

Besides this, we should be moved and drawn to prayer. For in addition to this commandment and promise, God expects us and He Himself arranges the words and form of prayer for us. He places them on our lips for how and what we should pray (Psalm 51:15), so that we may see how heartily He pities us in our distress (Psalm 4:1), and we may never doubt that such prayer is pleasing to Him and shall certainly be answered. This (the Lord's Prayer) is a great advantage indeed over all other prayers that we might compose ourselves. For in our own prayers the conscience would ever be in doubt and say, "I have prayed, but who knows if it pleases Him or whether I have hit upon the right proportions and form?" Therefore, there is no nobler prayer to be found upon earth than the Lord's Prayer. We pray it daily (Matthew 6:11), because it has this excellent testimony, that God loves to hear it. We ought not to surrender this for all the riches of the world.

The Lord's Prayer has also been prescribed so that we should see and consider the distress that ought to drive and compel us to pray without ceasing (1 Thessalonians 5:17). For whoever would pray must have something to present, state, and name, which he desires. If he does not, it cannot be called a prayer.

We have rightly rejected the prayers of monks and priests, who howl and growl day and night like fiends. But none of them think of praying for a hair's breadth of anything. If we would assemble all the churches, together with all churchmen, they would be bound to confess that they have never from the heart prayed for even a drop of wine. For none of them has ever intended to pray from obedience to God and faith in His promise. No one has thought about any need. But when they had done their best they thought no further than this: To do a good work, by which they might repay God. They were unwilling to take anything from Him, but wished only to give Him something.

But where there is to be a true prayer, there must be seriousness. People must feel their distress, and such distress presses them and compels them to call and cry out. Then prayer will be made willingly, as it ought to be. People will need no teaching about how to prepare for it and to reach the proper devotion. But the distress that ought to concern us most (both for ourselves and everyone), you will find abundantly set forth in the Lord's Prayer. Therefore, this prayer also serves as a reminder, so that we meditate on it and lay it to heart and do not fail to pray. For we all have enough things that we lack. The great problem is that we do not feel or recognize this. Therefore, God also requires that you weep and ask for such needs and wants, not because He does not know about them (Matthew 6:8), but so that you may kindle your heart to stronger and greater desires and make wide and open your cloak to receive much (Psalm 10:17).

Every one of us should form the daily habit from his youth of praying for all his needs. He should pray whenever he notices anything affecting his interests or that of other people among whom he may live. He should pray for preachers, the government, neighbors, household servants, and always (as we have said) to hold up to God His commandment and promise, knowing that He will not have them disregarded. This I say because I would like to see these things brought home again to the people so that they might learn to pray truly and not go about coldly and indifferently. They become daily more unfit for prayer because of indifference. That is just what the devil desires, and for which he works with all his powers. He is well aware what damage and harm it does him when prayer is done properly.

We need to know this: all our shelter and protection rest in prayer alone. For we are far too weak to deal with the devil and all his power and followers who set themselves against us. They might easily crush us under their feet. Therefore, we must consider and take up those weapons with which Christians must be armed in order to stand against the devil (2 Corinthians 10:4; Ephesians 6:11). For what do you imagine has done such great things up till now? What has stopped or quelled the counsels, purposes, murder, and riot of our enemies, by which the devil thought he would crush us, together with the Gospel? It was the prayer of a few godly people standing in the middle like an iron wall for our side. Otherwise they would have witnessed a far different tragedy. They would have seen how the devil would have destroyed all Germany in its own blood. But now our enemies may confidently ridicule prayer and make a mockery of it. However, we shall still be a match both for them and the devil by prayer alone, if we only persevere diligently and do not become slack. For whenever a godly Christian prays, "Dear Father, let Your will be done" (see Matthew 6:10), God speaks from on high and says, "Yes, dear child, it shall be so, in spite of the devil and all the world." (15–32)

Glossary

antinomianism. The teaching that the Law has no place in Christian proclamation or in the life of the believer. This view was championed by John Agricola at the time of the Reformation. It was rejected by both Luther and the Lutheran Confessions as it ultimately turned the Gospel into a new law.

cafeterianism. An attempt to create one's own worldview by selecting, cafeteria-style, religious or moral concepts, ideas, and practices from a variety of sources. A person who attends a Christian church on Sunday while believing in reincarnation might be viewed as a "cafeterian," for example, since bodily resurrection and reincarnation are inherently incompatible.

Deus absconditus. The hidden God or God as He hides Himself.

Deus revelatus. The revealed God or God as He reveals Himself in Christ.

Darwinism. An explanation for the existence and diversity of life on earth, attributed to Charles Darwin, which includes such concepts as evolution, natural selection ("survival of the fittest"), adaptation, and other concepts.

doxology. Although not appearing in the text of the Lord's Prayer, a traditional ending recited at the conclusion of it: "For Thine is the kingdom and the power and the glory forever and ever."

Enthusiasts. A term used by Luther to refer to the radical spiritualists who believed that God came to them without the external instruments of Word and Sacrament.

Evangelicalism. Rooted in the American revivalist movements of the eighteenth and nineteenth centuries, modern Evangelicalism is typified by a strong belief in biblical inerrancy, Christ's work on the cross as the only means of man's forgiveness, an emphasis on personal conversion, and the centrality of evangelism in congregational and personal life.

fundamentalism. A movement in the late nineteenth and twentieth centuries that stressed the inspiration and inerrancy of the Bible over and against Darwinism and other aspects of Enlightenment thought.

Gospel reductionism. Using the Gospel to suggest considerable latitude in faith and life not explicitly detailed in the Gospel.

historical critical method. An approach to the study of the Scriptures shaped by Enlightenment presuppositions regarding history and the accessibility of historical events to the interpreter. Those who practiced this method more often than not denied the divine character of the Scriptures.

hours of prayer. Set times and customs of prayer rooted in early Christian practice: matins, lauds, prime, terce, sext, none, vespers, compline. (Matins and lauds were combined in some traditions.) Lutheran hymnals often contain services for matins (morning service) and vespers (evening service).

humanism. A broad range of philosophies that emphasize human dignity and worth and recognize a common morality based on universal, rational human nature. Humanists who deny the possibility of any supernatural involvement in human affairs are sometimes called *secular* humanists.

intercession. Prayer offered on behalf of another person or persons.

liturgical prayer. Prayers offered in the sacrificial part of the Church's public worship (hymns, collects, prayers, Preface, *Sanctus*, Lord's Prayer, *Agnus Dei*, canticles, etc.).

Lord's Prayer. Prayer taught by Jesus (see Matthew 6:9–13; Luke 11:2–4). In some Christian traditions, also called the "Our Father," after the prayer's introduction.

modernism. A cultural movement emerging in the late 1800s and later emphasizing the inevitability of human achievement (especially through science and technology) and a positive view of human reason, particularly in its ability to determine the truth.

mysticism. While mysticism itself is a brand of spirituality with distinct nuances, it is best characterized by the movement to transcend or move above the earthly through inward experience.

postmodernism. Refers to a cluster of ideas arising in the 1920s and later uniformly opposed to the objective claims of *modernism.* The focus of postmodernism is characterized by pluralism, the rejection of the concept of absolute truth, as well as the denial of "meta-narratives," or comprehensive attempts to explain anything.

oratio, meditatio, tentatio. Prayer, meditation, and trial. Luther said that theologians (students of God's Word) are made by prayer, meditation, and the trial of life under the cross.

rationalism. The Enlightenment movement that sees human reason as the ultimate criterion for reality rather than religious dogma.

reductionism. A *modern* concept focusing on the human ability to reduce complex ideas or things to simple or more fundamental ideas or things. *Fundamentalism* exhibits reductionism in its attempt to reduce the Christian faith to very few "key" concepts or teachings. *Gospel reductionism* makes a similar error by devaluing or outright rejecting God's Law in the life of the believer (see also *antinomianism*).

sola scriptura. Scripture alone. Scripture is the singular fountain of Christian teaching and the final rule by which to evaluate all proclamation in the Church.